Teron V. Gaddis

To Judge Barley
Keep Praying God's
Words !

Pastor

Senior Editor: Ramona Y. Dindy

Edited by: Jamila M. Woodard

Cover design: Jamar Patterson

Author photo: Leland Tucker

To the love of my life, my parents, grandparents, my pastors, and the people I have had the privilege of pastoring for 25 years. Your investment into my life has made all the difference in the world to me one verse at a time, one sermon at a time.

Foreword(s)

Pastor John A. Reed, Jr., Senior Pastor
Fairview Baptist Church, Oklahoma City, OK

Pastor Teron (Terry) Gaddis received and accepted the call to the Gospel Ministry while growing and developing in Christian discipleship at the Fairview Baptist Church where I have had the privilege of serving as Pastor for the past fifty-four years. He served as an associate Minister for a number of years before answering the call to Pastoral Ministry. During his tenure with the Fairview family, he often heard me make the statement to the congregation, "where there is prayer in the pew, there will be power in the pulpit." That statement was advice and counsel to our membership to pray for the Pastor. That was the challenge used by Pastor Gaddis in the writing of this book, Praying for our Pastors."

He is utilizing various practical means for implementing scriptural calls to prayer into the life of a local church. As their motivation to pray, God's people need to appreciate the importance of prayer. A right purpose and proper attitude should determine the manner of prayer.

In his book, Pastor Gaddis is training people to pray for our Pastors. He gives a biblical reference for praying for the pastor. At the root of it all is the need for each believer to realize that prayer is foundational; prayer is not supplemental. Believer's need to pray more often over the many issues in which our Pastors face daily. Praying must be a priority of the church. God is just waiting for His people to pray. Prayer moves the hand of God. Prayer makes the difference.

Thank you, Pastor Gaddis for reminding us that if we are going to experience the blessings on God can give, we as God's people must humble ourselves and pray, especially for our Pastors.

This book is a must – read for every believer.

Dr. Bryan Carter, Senior Pastor
Concord Church, Dallas, TX

I first came to know Pastor Gaddis about 15 years ago. Over this time, I have been honored to witness his dynamic leadership. He has lead Greater Bethel Church to be incredibly effective in serving the community. He has a high aptitude for reaching people in his own unique way. These skills allow him to be one of the leading pastors in the Oklahoma City area.

We can say with confidence that a key component to success in ministry is prayer. Jesus laid the foundation for what prayer looks like and its importance. He gave us a framework for how we should pray in Matthew 6:9-13. We should praise God, expressing our adoration. We should pray that His will is accomplished. We are to pray that daily needs are met. We also ask for help with our daily struggles. Jesus also acknowledged the need to be consistent in our prayers (Matthew 7:7-8). We are to pray with love, patience, wisdom, and an understanding that He will satisfy our needs. The early believers showed us the effectiveness of lifting our voices together to ask for help and strength to serve boldly, especially while facing challenges (Acts 4:24-30).

Prayer should be a staple for believers. In John Maxwell's book, *Partners in Prayer*, he emphasizes how we are to pray for others, including church leaders, noting the value that occurs when churches pray for their pastor. Considering the magnitude of a pastor's calling, believers should pray diligently for their leader. Specifically, pray for your pastor to (1) grow daily in His relationship with Christ, (2) be led away from temptation, (3) have a pure and loving heart, (4) have strength in service, (5) be healed from hurt and pain, (6) have protection, (7) have a thriving family, (8) be committed to the Great Commission.

When people would go to visit Charles Spurgeon's church, he made it a point to take them to the basement. There, the visitors would find people on their knees, offering intercessory prayers for the church. Spurgeon referred to this as "the powerhouse of the church". From my own perspective, I can attest to how a praying congregation has been monumental in ministry. This book is a timely publication in the age where people are being carried away by every wind of doctrine, while pastors are under constant spiritual attack. There is need for people to know how to pray the Word of God over their pastor and this book is a great tool in helping people to understand how to do so.

Your Pastor Needs You!

Charles Spurgeon says, "Prayer will singularly assist you in the delivery of your sermon. In Fact, nothing can so gloriously fit you to preach as descending fresh from the mount of communion with God to speak with men."

God is clear on the roles He has set in His Church. There are crystal clear responsibilities for pastor and parishioner, clergy and congregation, as well as pastor and pew. However, there is a huge misconception of the Pastor's role that leads to a delayed response from the pew.

Think about it. Everybody needs encouragement. As a parishioner, we know where to go when we are faced with the dark, disappointing, depressing and dreary days we all face. Have you ever wondered where the pastor goes, who the pastor talks to, and what the pastor does when he needs to be encouraged, strengthened and counseled?

In over 50 years of being on this earth, I have worked in entry level positions all the way to the second highest position in a fifteen-million-dollar corporation where nearly fifty employees reported directly to me. And by far, pastoring stands apart as the most difficult responsibility of them all. My successor, the late Dr. C. C. Cooper, pastored the Greater Bethel Church for over 35 years and I often must remind myself of his faithfulness to get me through some of the most trying days of ministry.

Whether you realize it or not our pastors are under attack. They are being attacked from within their own spirits, within their own congregations and from without by those who are being used by the enemy. Pastors often feel pain, have problems, and are persecuted. Pastors are often found praying for others, but have you ever asked who is praying for the Pastor. Pastors teach, preach, counsel, visit the sick, homebound, prisons, hospitals, schools, and homes pouring into others and are left empty almost every day.

So, what can you do for your Pastor? What does your Pastor need?

Pastors need someone who is on board, sees the vision, and is someone he can count on, lean on, and invest in. If you are interested this book is for you. Here are a few ideas you could put into action to stand alongside of your pastor:

1. **P**ray for your Pastor
2. **R**each out to your Pastor
3. **E**ncourage your Pastor
4. **A**ppreciate your Pastor
5. **C**atch the vision of your Pastor
6. **H**onestly share with your Pastor
7. Sit down with your Pastor
8. Serve alongside your Pastor

Why Pray for Your Pastor?

Beyond the struggles of the churches, most of, many of the pastors in the United States are struggling personally. The grind of the demands of the solo-pastor is burning American pastors out. Licensed professional counselor Michael Todd Wilson and veteran pastor Brad Hoffman report the following sobering statistics in their book Preventing Ministry Failure.

✝ 90 percent of American pastors surveyed feel inadequately trained to cope with ministry demands.

✝ 45 percent say they have experienced depression or burnout to the extent that they needed to take a leave of absence.

✝ Every month, 1,500 pastors leave the ministry permanently in America. Many more would leave if they could afford it. In a recent survey, more than 50 percent of pastors said they would leave their ministry if they could replace their income.

In their book Pastors at Greater Risk, H. B. London and Neil Wiseman quote startling statistics from research conducted by Fuller Theological Seminary. These statistics are the reflection of the trap of the "Lone Ranger" pastor.

- ✞ 80 percent of pastors say they have insufficient time with spouse and that ministry has a negative effect on their family.
- ✞ 40 percent report a serious conflict with a parishioner once a month.

- ✞ 75 percent report they have had a significant stress-related crisis at least once in their ministry.

- ✞ 45 percent of pastors' wives say the greatest danger to them and family is physical, emotional, mental, and spiritual burnout.

- ✞ 21 percent of pastors' wives want more privacy.

- ✞ Pastors who work fewer than fifty hours a week are 35 percent more likely to be terminated.

- ✠ 40 percent of pastors considered leaving the pastorate in the past three months.

- ✠ 25 percent of pastors' wives see their husband's work schedule as a source of conflict.

- ✠ 48 percent of pastors think being in ministry is hazardous to family well-being.

These statistics make it acutely aware to me while there may have been preaching going on in the pulpit there was a lack of praying going on in the pews. Many times, as a pastor I have been asked by my members, "Pastor what can I do for you?" And my answer has always been the same. "Pray for me."

Being a pastor is a dangerous profession. There is a commander-in-chief who has recruited generals (pastors) to get the necessary instruction and supplies to the troops and the enemy is doing everything he can to try and stop the dissemination of the information. So, when members become so bogged down in the ministry that they forget about the man of God, the mission is misguided. And this very thing is what is happening in our churches.

Several years ago, at one of the lowest points of my ministry I showed up to close out in prayer one Sunday morning with our Intercessory Prayer Warriors, and I just could not do it. Instead I begin to weep. I was depressed. The prayer warriors sensed what was going on with me and one by one they begin to pray. Later, I found out that their time together, every Sunday morning at 8:30 a.m., was not just to pray for the worship experience; but also for me.

Because of their praying I was able to fulfill my assignment for the day to "preach the Word!" From that day on, my heart opened to other pastors who had to stand every week with the same assignment. I went to my church and we began to pray for the pastors in our city, sending them cards and letters of encouragement. I begin to receive text messages and phone calls from those pastors saying, "Thank you for your prayers."

Only someone who is willfully ignorant could look at the modern church without seeing the problems pastors face. We operate in a world that is hostile to our message.

Financially, numerically, and spiritually, the 21st century church is in deep trouble. In most cities, the only churches growing are those who have embraced a worldlier atmosphere and message. Churches that still cling to the Word of God in their preaching and worship are dying at an alarming rate.

Pastors are not immune from trouble. They need God's help. That is why my team and I have put this book together. We may never know the specifics of how God answered our prayers while praying for the pastors of our state. We do, however, know and believe there is power in prayer.

Change could come about in our churches, our communities, our city, and even our country, if the people in the pews began to faithfully and fervently pray for the man of God. I have no doubt about the change.

I am asking that each week you pray not only for your pastor; but, you also pray for other pastors within your community. I believe that your obedience will cause a shift in the churches in this great country.

Praying from the Pews to Produce Productive and Powerful Pastors

Leonard Ravenhill says, "Preaching affects men; prayer affects God. Preaching affects time; prayer affects eternity."

In Exodus 18:14-18 we find these words.

"14 When Moses' father-in-law saw all that he was doing for the people, he said, "What is this that you are doing for the people? Why do you sit alone, and all the people stand around you from morning till evening?" 15 And Moses said to his father-in-law, "Because the people come to me to inquire of God; 16 when they have a dispute, they come to me and I decide between one person and another, and I make them know the statutes of God and his laws." 17 Moses' father-in-law said to him, "What you are doing is not good. 18 You and the people with you will certainly wear yourselves out, for the thing is too heavy for you. You are not able to do it alone.""

At this point in time in Moses' ministry he was experiencing spiritual amnesia. Thank God for Jethro, his father-in law. Jethro was a veteran shepherd who oversaw a massive herd. He noticed how Moses was leading the people and decided to give him some fatherly advice. Jethro's advice to Moses is what the people needed to understand then and what we need to understand today that pastors must do in ministry, not what they ought to do.

God had strategically placed Moses with Jethro for Moses to learn the trade of a shepherd firsthand. One of the things that Moses was taught was that a flock is too large for one shepherd to handle. The people were clamoring for help; however, no one was helping Moses. He was failing in trying the meet the needs of all the people as just one man. And this very thing is happening in churches across this country. Many times, pastors are trying to do the job of many being one. This method is the prescription for failure. The only result will be burnout. It is not the pastor's responsibility to handle the entire ministry. The pastor has a ministry and each member of the church has a ministry.

The average church size in America is about 75 – 100 people. In these churches, pastors are expending unnecessary energy to try to be everything to everyone. People are quick to point out the sin of the pastor. My question when these things are discovered, "What was the church doing?" When people talk about pastors' infidelity, pastors' embezzling funds, pastors with drug and alcohol problems, I must ask where was the church? This, of course, is not an excuse for their sin. This is a call for the church to step up and do her job of covering her shepherd. Just maybe the sin in the pulpit is a result of the sin in the pews. What sin am I referring to? The sin of not praying for the pastor.

Often it is the expectation of the pew that causes the vacating of the pulpit. While pastors believe they are coming to the church to pastor, they fail to examine the history that they are inheriting. They are unaware of the committee behind the committee. The ones who hold the meeting before the meeting. They are brought in with one set of goals based on the discussions with the pulpit search committee only to get there and discover that they were not called to pastor but to be a puppet. Some pastors come in on the heels of another pastor with hopes that one day the members will follow them as they follow God only to find out that they would forever live in the shadow of the one who served before them.

Dr. Joel Gregory in his book "No Greater Temptation" tells the story of his transition from the great pastor of the First Baptist Church, Dallas to a door-to-door insurance salesperson selling pre-need funeral plans for Greenwood Cemetery where he had performed numerous funerals, after a decision to resign at a Wednesday night service. This went on for several years Joel Gregory said and then one day God saw fit in 1997 for Dr. E. K. Bailey to invite Dr. Gregory to stand and proclaim the gospel at an expository preaching conference. It was at this conference that Dr. Gregory's call to the preaching ministry was resurrected. From that one preaching assignment in front of 900 predominately African-American preachers and pastors, of which I was a member of, Dr. Gregory begin to receive invitations to preach across the country. Dr. Gregory spoke that night from 2 Corinthians 4:6 referring to the brokenness in earthen vessels. Dr. Gregory used his own personal brokenness in ministry to encourage that predominately African American audience to continue in the preaching ministry. While it had been said that he would always be known as the pastor who resigned from the largest Baptist church in America, now he was known as the one who stood Sunday after Sunday, rightly dividing the Word of truth.

We unveiled the problem in verses 14-18. Now let's consider the solution. In looking at the story of Moses and Jethro I want to teach you what the God-given responsibility of the pastor is by starting off by taking the backdoor approach and teaching you what the pastor's responsibility is not.

The pastor is not called to be a counselor, career coach, business adviser, custodian, arbitrator, social worker, volunteer coordinator, event manager, fundraiser, recruiter, trainer, writer, manager public relations, wedding coordinator, song leader, and marriage counselor, referee or day care worker.

I am so grateful for the Word of God because I did not have to make up these things based on my own personal experiences. It is in the Word of God that we find three very important things that the pastor's God-given responsibility. What greater reference to have than the inspired Word of God.

I want to put a quick footnote here. You might want to underline it or even rewrite it in the margin because it will definitely bless you. A church never calls a pastor.

In verse 19 of Exodus chapter 18, listen to the words of Jethro. **"Now obey my voice; I will give you advice, and God be with you! You shall represent the people before God and bring their cases to God,"**

Before we go any further, I want to ask you to read those words again. What do those instructions sound like? They sound like instructions to pray. The pastor's first responsibility is to be a PRAY-ER. The pastor's responsibility is to intercede for the people. The pastor's responsibility is to spend time with God enough where God can tell him what the people need. If the pastor is performing all these other duties when does he have time to pray for you? How is he supposed to receive a word from God on your behalf and truly care for you if he is not praying for you?

I recall some very sage advice from my spiritual mentor, Pastor A. Glenn Woodberry regarding midnight phone calls from members whose loved ones have gone on to glory. Pastor Woodberry said to me, "Son, the greatest thing you can do for the family at that point is to pray. God has already done His part, now do what you have been called to do. Pray for the family."

Not only is the pastor's responsibility to pray, his responsibility is also to be a PREACH-ER. Verse 20 in Exodus chapter 18 says, **"and you shall warn them about the statutes and the laws, and make them know the way in which they must walk and what they must do."** God is holding each of us responsible for God's law. And it is the pastor's responsibility to rightly divide the Word of God so that it becomes profitable for teaching, for reproof, for correction, and for sound training in righteousness. *(2 Timothy 3:16)* The pastor's responsibility is to stand boldly behind that sacred desk to proclaim the gospel. If every time you leave the church house you are smiling, then there is a good chance that you are listening to someone who is not 'warning you about the statutes and the laws'. There is a good chance that you are not listening to someone who is letting you know the 'way in which you must walk and what you must do'.

It is the pastor's responsibility to pray, to preach, and finally it is the pastor's responsibility to be a PREPARE-ER. Verse 21 in Exodus chapter 18 says, **"Moreover, look for able men from all the people, men who fear God, who are trustworthy and hate a bribe, and place such men over the people as chiefs of thousands, of hundreds, of fifties, and of tens."** The pastor's responsibility is to equip the church to do the work of ministry. His responsibility is not to take on the ministry. The pastor's responsibility is to ensure that the church is growing and becoming productive citizens in the kingdom of God. The pastor's responsibility is to make sure that all the limbs of the body is functioning properly. God designed it that He is the head of the church and He then called pastors to earthly leadership. If the head is not functioning properly then neither will the limbs. It is the head that houses the central nervous system. The central nervous system controls the functions of the body, not to do all the work but to send the necessary messages to the limbs so that they learn to function properly on their own.

Therefore, we must pray for the pastor. We must pray for the pastor so that he does not become weary. We must pray for the pastor so that he does not become worn out. We must pray for the pastor so that he does not have to worry. We must pray for the pastor because one of his primary responsibilities is to pray for us and we want him to adequately be able to do so.

A Biblical Reference for
Praying for the Pastor
Acts 12

At the time of our text the church had experienced unbelievable growth through the power of God moving in miraculous ways. 3,000 people were saved on one occasion *(Acts 2:41)*. 5,000 were saved on another occasion *(Acts 4:4)*. The early church was marked by the manifest power and presence of God through the preaching of His Word that produced peace and harmony within the church and souls being saved daily. The people were excited, equipped, encouraged and enlightened through the apostles teaching and preaching. The power of God's Word was working. The church was growing. God was worshipped. The people belonged. Scripture was studied. Saints served. The story of Jesus was shared and sinners were being saved. It was a great time to be a part of the church!

But, not everyone was pleased! The Jews hated the early church because the church said that Jesus was the Messiah. The Jews were guilty of killing Him and to make matters worse they claimed to be eyewitnesses of Jesus' resurrection. It wasn't long before the church came under fire from enemies.

The Jewish leaders had tried everything to quiet the message of Jesus being raised from the dead. They put out a rumor that His body was stolen. They arrested the Apostles forbidding them to preach the Gospel. And yet, they stood boldly and spoke truth in power and said they would not stop. So, after the rumors and the threats, they put a hit out. They arrested Stephen, tried him and stoned him to death to frighten and possibly freeze the tremendous and unprecedented growth of the church *(Acts 6:8-7:60)*. However, every attempt to slow down and eventually stop the spread of the Gospel of Jesus Christ failed. They used hired guns like Saul of Tarsus; but he ended up being saved. They persecuted the saints and many members of the church were scattered to the ends of the earth. Still, the church continued to gain power, prosperity, and people.

That brings us to Acts 12.

Acts 12:1-5 says, ¹"About that time Herod the king laid violent hands on some who belonged to the church. ²He killed James the brother of John with the sword, ³and

when he saw that it pleased the Jews, he proceeded to arrest Peter also. This was during the days of Unleavened Bread. ⁴And when he had seized him, he put him in prison, delivering him over to four squads of soldiers to guard him, intending after the Passover to bring him out to the people. ⁵So Peter was kept in prison, but earnest prayer for him was made to God by the church.

Pastor Peter was preaching Jesus, honoring the Lord, and trouble still came his way.

There is a lesson here for us as well in this text. We must never get the idea that a good, godly life is a hedge against *We must never get the idea that a good, godly life is a hedge against troubles.* troubles. Sometimes, the closer one lives to Jesus the more that person suffers for Jesus. Just a quick rundown of the men of God in the Bible whose lives are testaments and testimonies of the suffering saints, lonely leaders, chastised champions, persecuted and unappreciated prophets, sad and sorrowful servants. Men like Moses, Jeremiah, Elijah, Elisha, David, Paul and even the Lord Jesus. Jesus is called "a man of sorrows" *(Isaiah.*

53:3). If Jesus suffered trials and setbacks in life; we should expect no better treatment ourselves.

Peter discovered this when he was thrown into Herod's prison. But, it was in prison Pastor Peter experienced the power of God as the people of God bombarded heavens gates on behalf of their pastor.

We pray a lot, but I fear we fail to pray for our pastor. We pray for our needs, our burdens, our bumps, our bruises, our family, our faith, our finances, our marriages, our children and our health but how much time do we really spend praying for our pastor?

Right now, there are pastors who are standing in pulpits across this country on the verge of giving up, throwing in the towel, filing for divorce, committing suicide, becoming alcoholics, giving in to drug addiction, pornography, homosexuality, and even abuse. We should be touching Heaven for them. Their marriage has crashed. We should be touching Heaven for them. Pastors children have become crushed by unsympathetic congregations that have been cold and callus to them and their parents. We should be touching Heaven for them. There are pastors who deal with uncooperative boards. We should be touching Heaven for them. Our leaders are struggling with money, memories, miseries and mistakes. We should be touching Heaven for them. They are imprisoned by failures, and fears; anguish and anger; problems and pains, the evil one and the evildoers, unfaithful, unconcerned and uninvolved memberships. We should be touching Heaven for them. They need you to touch Heaven for them!

There is a tiny word in Acts 12:5 that makes a big difference. It is the little conjunction "but". The situation looks desperate, BUT! It looks as though Peter might be put to death, BUT! It looks as though the fledgling church might be destroyed before it can carry the Gospel to the world, BUT! In the face of overwhelming problems, the church bowed its head as one person and it called on God for their pastor. The church did not cower in fear before those who threatened them. The church lifted its collective voice and rang heaven's door bells! God heard their prayers and moved by His mighty power and answered the church's prayer! Let's examine their prayer, because it is the kind of prayer we should be offering up as a church for our pastor(s).

The church went down on their knees in fervent prayer for their pastor. We are told "prayer was made without ceasing…" The word "ceasing" means "to stretch forth". It is a medical term that refers to a stretched ligament or a pulled muscle. It has the idea of "going beyond the boundaries". When applied to prayer, it is a picture of fervency. It is the picture of people pouring out their hearts in prayer before the Lord as they seek His face for their needs.

That's the kind of praying we need to undertake. The promise of God is "the effectual fervent prayer of a righteous men availeth much" *(James 5:16)*. The words "effectual fervent" refer to "energetic passionate" prayer. It is not prayer that is sluggish, lifeless, unconcerned, casual, halfhearted, blasé or apathetic. It is prayer that pours forth from a burdened heart. It is the kind of prayer that reaches heaven and moves the hand of God.

The church not only went down in fervent prayer, but they also went down on their knees in faith-filled prayer for their pastor. By faithful praying, I mean theirs was a prayer of faith. Their prayers were made "to God". This seems obvious, but there are times when it seems like our prayers are designed to be heard by other people, or even by us. This congregation joined their voices and reached up as one to touch God for their church and for Peter. When we pray, we must pray in faith. Faith is the essential ingredient that marks the difference between answered and unanswered prayer.

The Bible makes these statements about the role of faith in prayer:

Hebrew 11:6 "And without faith it is impossible to please him, for whoever would draw near to God must believe that he exists and that he rewards those who seek him."

Matthew 21:22 "And whatever you ask in prayer, you will receive, if you have faith."

1 John 5:14-15 "[14]And this is the confidence that we have toward him, that if we ask anything according to his will he hears us. [15]And if we know that he hears us in whatever we ask, we know that we have the requests that we have asked of him."

Luke 22:31-32 [31]**"Simon, Simon, behold, Satan demanded to have you, that he might sift you like wheat,** [32] **but I have prayed for you that your faith may not fail. And when you have turned again, strengthen your brothers."**

In addition to fervent and faith-filled prayer, the church went down on their knees in focused prayer for their pastor. Prayer was "made...for him". In other words, Peter was the focus of this prayer meeting. They came together to pray for a specific purpose. This was not generalized praying, that sought to cast a big blanket of prayer over everything and everyone. This was pointed prayer that sought God's power for a specific need.

If we do not pray specific prayers, how will we ever know when God answers? When we ask Him for specific needs, and God answers, it glorifies Him, it assures us of our relationship to Him, and it increases our faith. All I am suggesting is we need to get specific in our praying!

And finally, the church went down on their knees in family prayer for their pastor. The church gathered together to pray for their pastor, their preacher, their leader. They came together as a family to seek God's help for the pastor's greatest need. The church touched Heaven for Pastor Peter.

Their prayers had power because they were united in fervent prayer, faith-filled prayer, focused prayer and family prayer to God. They joined their hearts and their hands and then lifted their voices to God in prayer for the man of God so the Word of God would continue to go into all the world. God heard them and moved in power and Pastor Peter was delivered.

Why We Should Pray for our Pastor

John Bunyan says, "Pray often, for prayer is a shield to the soul, a sacrifice to God, and a scourge for Satan."

1 Thessalonians 5:12-13 says, [12] *"We ask you, brothers, to respect [Appreciate] those who [diligently] labor among you and are over you in the Lord and admonish you [give you instruction],* [13] *and to esteem them very highly in love because of their work. Be at peace among yourselves."* As people of God, we must understand when we neglect the man of God we are hurting ourselves.

We all love blessings.

We love it especially when God is pouring out His blessings on us.

We all enjoy the times when God is working in our lives and it is evident His power and presence are being manifested.

Yet there is something we all need to understand about the times of blessings.

Blessings are always followed by battles.

• Blessings are always followed by

battles.

- The smile of God is always followed by the snarl of the devil.
- The hour of triumph is always followed by the hour of testing.
- Prosperity is always followed by adversity.

There are several examples of this truth in the Scripture. One scene illustrates this point is the baptism of the Lord Jesus. In **Matthew 3:16-17** we read, *¹⁶ And when Jesus was baptized, immediately he went up from the water, and behold, the heavens were opened to him, and he saw the Spirit of God descending like a dove and coming to rest on him; ¹⁷ and behold, a voice from heaven said, "This is my beloved Son, with whom I am well pleased."*

That was a glorious hour because all persons of the trinity were involved and manifested themselves. There was Jesus standing in the river Jordan. The Holy Spirit descended like a dove upon Him and then the voice of the Father was heard. Wouldn't it have been nice to have been there at that special moment?

It is, however, in the very next verse we see the other side of the coin. **Matthew 4:1** says,

¹ Then Jesus was led up by the Spirit into the wilderness to be tempted by the devil. My hermeneutics professor taught us that, "When you find a *'then'* in the Bible look for the *'when'*."

When Jesus was baptized **then** the snarls of the devil were heard. The blessing of his baptism was followed by the battle that challenged his boldness.

Another example we find in the Bible of this concept is Elijah on Mount Carmel. That was a great hour in Elijah's life as he stood face to face and toe to toe with the 450 worshippers of Baal. God answered his prayer through fire proving Himself to be God. I am sure the result had Elijah on a mountaintop spiritually, as well as, physically.

But *no sooner* than the embers cooled, Jezebel issued a death warrant for his life. Elijah went from the heights of Carmel to the depths of the wilderness, lying under a juniper tree wishing to die. Once again there was a blessing that was soon followed by a battle.

Let's take a deeper look at this principle in Exodus 17. The first scene begins in verse 8.

Exodus 17:8 *"⁸ Then Amalek came and fought with Israel at Rephidim."*

Remember I mentioned earlier what I learned from my hermeneutics professor? Here is that concept again. There is a little word you cannot miss in this verse *"then"* or it may read in your version *"now."* Up until now several things had happened to the Jewish people.

First, there was the encounter with the Red Sea. It was meant to stop them. However, God pushed the wall down and turned it into a bridge and delivered the people from Egyptian bondage.

Then the children of Israel came to a place in the wilderness called Marah. It was an oasis of water and they were dying of thirst. They tasted the waters and the waters were bitter and undrinkable. When God put his finger in the water and turned it into the sweetest water on earth.

Then they came to a place called Elim. Here they were starving to death because they had no food. And again, when God came through and began to rain down manna from heaven until their stomachs were full.

So here we are in the first part of this chapter, where we see the children of Israel came to a place called Rephidim. Again, they were dying of thirst. This time there was absolutely no water, bitter or sweet. God told Moses to strike a rock in Horeb with his rod and water would come forth. Moses did just that and a rock became a fountain of fresh water. The singular point I am making, up until this point is Israel had been given blessing after blessing after blessing.

Then the text says, *"Then Amalek came and fought with Israel in Rephidim."*

Now it is important to understand who Amalek is.

Amalek was the grandson of Esau. If you remember, Esau was the man who sold his birthright for a mess of pottage. His descendants became the first nation to oppose Israel after they left Egypt.

"Then Amalek came and fought with Israel in Rephidim."

Now let me go ahead and clue you in. In the Bible, Amalek represents the flesh; not the physical flesh, but the sinful nature we are born with that causes us to do bad when we want to do good.

It is interesting that whenever you read about Amalek, he is always found inside the camp of Israel. This fact is a direct correlation to the enemy inside of us called the flesh. You all know we have three enemies: the world, the devil, and the flesh.

I am convinced that the greatest enemy is not the devil; the greatest enemy is the flesh. Because neither the world nor the devil can get to us except through the flesh.

There is no record the Jews ever had to fight any battle in Egypt. But once they were delivered from bondage, the enemies began to line up. That is exactly the way it is in the Christian life. When you are born again, the battle begins.

Now the Lord is our Giver of Blessings, and from the moment we are saved, we become heirs to all the blessings of God. But remember this along with the blessings we receive we are also recipients of battles.

I would advise you not to view this as a bad thing but a good thing. It is good because God can use those battles to force us to trust the Giver rather than the gifts. He wants us to realize it is not necessarily bad to have to face enemies. It is not bad to have to fight battles. It is not necessarily bad to have the enemy wage war against us.

Why not? Because it keeps us alert. It keeps us vigilant. It makes us strong.

Now I want us to take a look at the next verse in chapter 17.

Exodus 17:9 *"⁹ So Moses said to Joshua, "Choose for us men, and go out and fight with Amalek. Tomorrow I will stand on the top of the hill with the staff of God in my hand."* Now why did Moses choose to go up to the hill?

From the hill, Moses would be able to see the bigger picture. He would get the best view. He would be able to see all angles of the battle. He would be able to see where the army was strongest and where they were the weakest.

Another good reason is that any good military man will tell you whoever has the higher ground always has the upper hand and the strategic advantage in any battle.

At this point, Moses represents the praying pastor. Joshua represents where you and I live and fight daily. Notice the pastor is praying while the people are fighting.

Exodus 17:10 says, *"¹⁰ So Joshua did as Moses told him, and fought with Amalek, while Moses, Aaron, and Hur went up to the top of the hill."*

Again, I need to remind you that while Moses (the pastor in the pulpit) is praying, Joshua (the people in the pews) is fighting.

You see if you go to war and don't pray you are a fool. And if you go to war without praying, you will fail.

There is a popular saying circulating through social media that says, "We ought to pray as if everything depends upon God, and we ought to work as if everything depends upon us."

Right now, I need you to listen very carefully! In fact, I need you to read these words out loud.

You cannot win…

- The fight in the valley unless your pastor is winning on the hilltop.
- The battle where you live unless your pastor is winning where he is.
- The war in pews, unless your pastor is winning in the pulpit.

Also…
- Weariness in prayer means weakness in battle.
- Weariness in the pews means weariness in the pulpit.
- Where the battle is really won or lost depends on prayer.

This story is fascinating. **Exodus 17:11 says,** *"¹¹ Whenever Moses held up his hand, Israel prevailed, and whenever he lowered his hand, Amalek prevailed."* When Moses raised his rod, Israel prevailed. Now, the word *"prevail"* in the Hebrew language literally means *"to be given strength,"* or *"to increase in strength."*

Whenever Moses held up his hand, Israel prevailed, and whenever he lowered his hand, Amalek prevailed.
Exodus 17:11

You see, prayer not only blesses you, it strengthens the people you are praying for. Therefore, it is so important you pray for other people.

Read verse 11 again carefully. Let's see if you notice what I noticed when I read it. We expect the first part of the verse to be true; that when Moses held up his hand, Israel prevailed. However, you would expect the second part of the verse to read, "When Moses lowered his hands, Israel did not prevail." But that is not what it says. It says when Moses "let down his hand Amalek prevailed." Do you know what that means? It means when we don't pray, we not only weaken ourselves, we strengthen the enemy. Please don't miss that. When you don't pray you not only take strength from yourself, you give strength to the devil, to the world, and to the flesh.

Prayer is not just a defensive weapon, it is also an offensive weapon. If you read Ephesians 6 about the armor of God, you will find that every single part of the armor is for defense except two; the sword of the spirit, which is the word of God, and prayer.

I want you to notice Joshua could not have succeeded without Moses. And Moses could not have prevailed without the support of an Aaron and a Hur. Moses got tired. He got weary. He needed men to come alongside of him to hold up his hands as he held up the rod of God.

Not everybody can be a Moses or a Joshua or a Billy Graham. But every Christian can be an Aaron or a Hur, holding up the arms of men of God. We must always remember Christian leaders desperately need our support in prayer.

That's why we need a call to arms. We need a call to pray for our pastors. You see, if there is no Hur and there is no Aaron, then Moses fails. And if Moses fails, Joshua fails. And if Joshua fails, Israel fails. And if Israel fails, the entire battle is lost.

Notice the results of Moses' victory in *Exodus 17:13*. Verse 13 says, **"And Joshua overwhelmed Amalek and his people with the sword"** It was not Moses who was empowering Joshua and his army. It was God who was empowering Moses and Joshua; both through prayer. One on the hilltop; the other in the valley. One in the prayer closet, one in the field of battle. And both together through the sovereign power of Almighty God.

The battle was not won because of Joshua's genius. The battle was not won because of the army's might. It was won on the hilltop through the power of prayer. Vigilance on the hilltop brings victory in the valley. I want to tell you, apart from prayer and the power that prayer brings, it doesn't matter how many buildings you build, how much of a budget you can raise, or how many benefits you can give, it will all come to ruin without god. Because when you work you see what you can do, but when you pray you see what God can do.

Vigilance on the hilltop brings victory in the valley.

Pastors are under attack today in every denomination and in every country. They are attacked from within their own churches by disgruntled attendees, within their own spirits by our enemy the devil, and from those who don't even attend or aren't members of the churches pastors have the privilege and responsibility to lead. The only way we can ward off the attacks of the enemy is when the people come together and began to pray. The type of prayer I am referring to cannot be an afterthought. It must be a forethought. We must decide as Christians to pray for our pastors continuously and without ceasing. The attacks they face do not stop, and neither should our prayers.

Pastors are under attack today in every denomination and in every country.

The Benefits of Praying for our Pastors

Martin Luther says, Prayer is a strong wall and fortress of the church; it is a goodly Christian weapon.

God is a God of order. Not only do Pastors certainly have a responsibility to the people in the pews; people also have some responsibility toward the pastor from the pews that cannot be discharged, denied or dismissed.

We should pray for our pastors because they are God's *"gracious gift"* to the church not a *"booby prize!"* **Jeremiah 3:15 says, *"And I will give you shepherds [Pastors] after my own heart, who will feed you with knowledge and understanding."*** God has given us Pastors to strengthen us, mature us, encourage us, feed us, lead us, and instruct us in our spiritual lives and to encourage our maturity in the faith.

As Christians, we should pray that our Pastors are Joyful. Hebrews 13:7 says, *"Remember your leaders, those who spoke to you the word of God. Consider the*

outcome of their way of life, and imitate their faith."

There are several things we must remember when it comes to our pastors.
1. We must be mindful of our pastors.

The church is commanded to *"remember your leaders"* in Hebrews 13:7. The word *"remember"* means, *"to be mindful of; to keep in mind; to think of and feel for a person; to make mention of."*

Let's take a moment to consider what it means for a church to be *"mindful"* or to *"remember"* the Pastor.

We must be mindful of our pastors.

We must 'Be mindful that your Pastor is God's man but he is still a man'!

The church is commanded *"to be thoughtful of the pastor."* This is a call for God's people to be considerate of their Pastor. God did not call the pastor to be at your beck and call. He called him and then sent him to the church to feed your souls and to lead you deeper in the things of God.

47

I believe too many church members and churches have forsaken the Pastor because they have forgotten that the Pastor is a person, a human, flesh and blood.

Some of the reasons we need to be considerate of the pastor is pastors shepherd dumb sheep that will walk over a cliff to their death, step on a piousness snake that could kill them, eat with their heads down right into being eaten themselves.

The challenge for you is to be considerate of your pastor.

- Give him time with his family.
- Give him time for personal and private prayer.
- Give him time to study of the Word of God.
- Encourage him with your words, thoughts and deeds.

Remember that:
- His load is lonesome.
- His road is rough.
- His time is tight.
- His temptation is tough.
- His pillow is wet.

- His heart is sometimes broken.

There will be times when he will be away from his family because he loves you.

There will be times when he will shoulder your burdens and carry them to the throne of grace and do spiritual battle on your behalf.

When he makes a mistake, forgive him.

When he falls, help him get back up again.

When we learn to carry our pastors in our hearts, God will bless their ministry.

We must 'Be mindful that your Pastor is God's man and he has feelings'.

'Be mindful that your Pastor is God's man and he has feelings'. The church is commanded *"to think of and to feel for the pastor"* — If you know what you face day in and day out – simply be mindful that your pastor must face those challenges and much more.

Learn to treat your Pastor like you would want to be treated. Take care of him. Supply his needs, after all that is God's command to the church.

1 Timothy 5:17 says, *"Let the elders who rule well be considered worthy of double honor, especially those who labor in preaching and teaching."*

Galatians 6:6 says, *"Let the one who is taught the word share all good things with the one who teaches."*

- Come by with a word of encouragement every now and then.

- Let him know you love him and are standing with him in the battle.

- Be a friend to the man of God!

- Have a heart for what your Pastor faces and remember that very often, his load will be heavier than your load.

- Why is his load heavier? Because he carries his burdens and he carries yours as well.

When you think of your Pastor and his family, always show him kindness. God will honor your efforts to be a friend to the man of God.

We must 'Be mindful that your Pastor is God's man and he still needs prayer'.
The church is commanded to *"to make mention of the pastor"*!

This is a call to the church to lift the man of God up in prayer.

One of the greatest gifts you can give to your pastor is the gift of your consistent, constant, and heart-felt prayers.

'Be mindful that your Pastor is God's man and he still needs prayer'.

Being the Pastor of a church is one of the greatest undertaking of his life.

Being the Pastor of a church is a responsibility greater than any man can bear alone.

He needs you to stand with him and to hold up his hands in prayer.

Just as Aaron and Hur stood with Moses, held up his hands, and thus enabled him to minister to all the people, those who sacrifice their time in prayer for their Pastor enable him to be a better servant of the Lord and the Lord's people.

When you pray for him, you will reap the benefit through his ministry of the Word of God.

When you pray for him, he will be empowered and God will use him to lead, feed and bless your church, your family and your life.

I'm not saying that prayer is your pastor's only need. I'm saying that when you pray you can better take care of his financial and material needs as well. That is why you must take the time to pray for him!

When you go into your prayer closet, don't forget to lift-up his name in prayer.

Know that when you pray for your pastor, God will honor that kind of sacrifice.

Every duty in the church should not rest upon the Pastor's shoulders. Get under the load of the work with him and the Lord will accomplish great things. Leave it all on the

Pastor's shoulders and not much will be accomplished!

Did you know the pastor's primary duty centers around prayer and the proclamation of the Word of God? (Application: *Acts 6:1-7* tells us the office of deacon was designed to be an extension of the Pastor's ministry.)

Acts 6:2-7 (ESV) *[2]"And the twelve summoned the full number of the disciples and said, "It is not right that we should give up preaching the word of God to serve tables. [3] Therefore, brothers, pick out from among you seven men of good repute, full of the Spirit and of wisdom, whom we will appoint to this duty. [4] But we will devote ourselves to prayer and to the ministry of the word." [5] And what they said pleased the whole gathering, and they chose Stephen, a man full of faith and of the Holy Spirit, and Philip, and Prochorus, and Nicanor, and Timon, and Parmenas, and Nicolaus, a proselyte of Antioch. [6] These they set before the apostles, and they prayed and laid their hands on them. [7] And the word of God continued to increase, and the number of the disciples multiplied greatly in*

Jerusalem, and a great many of the priests became obedient to the faith. "

Don't be guilty of being a burden to your pastor. Instead I encourage you to be a blessing. The job of the pastor is enormous and there should be a shared responsibility between the pulpit and the pews. Share the load as a greeter, usher, deacon, trustee, choir member, and member so that the ministry of the kingdom of God can go forward.

2. We must be respectful of our pastors.

Let's look at Hebrews 13:7 again.

"Remember your leaders [which have the rule over you... (KJV)]*, those who spoke to you the word of God. Consider the outcome of their way of life, and imitate their faith. "*

Here we are encouraged and commanded to be mindful of our pastor, as well as to be respectful of them. The word *"rule"* is used in the King James version and the word *"leaders,"* is used in the English Standard version of the Bible. The word *"rule"* refers to *"leadership"*. The word speaks of the authority, influence, and weight God has placed in the office of the Pastor. The trouble is many people who are members of the church have a difficult time accepting and aligning themselves up with the pastoral authority God has given the office of Pastor.

There are several reasons why people have a difficult time accepting the authority of the pastor.

One reason is there are pastors, tele-evangelists especially, that have misused and mistreated the office, operations and the obligation of the pastors. They have moved away from the primary responsibility of the pastor which is to lead, feed, encourage, keep and to mature the sheep of God.

It is imperative to stop here, long enough to do a bit of word study on the phrase *"have the rule over you"*. We must first understand that it is in the *passive voice*. In other words, these rulers are not in their positions by personal choice, but by the call and will of God. And, the phrase *"...those who spoke to you the word of God..." is a qualifying phrase that tell us who we are ought to respect.* He is talking about men of God who preach God's Word to God's people and is faithful to biblical hermeneutics.

So, what must I be respectful of?

I must be respectful of my pastor's rank.

Nature teaches us that living organisms only have one head. When an animal is born with two heads, it is called a "*freak*". The late Pastor A. G. Woodberry, would often say it this way, "anything with two heads is a 'freak' and there is nothing 'freakish' about God's Church." The church of Jesus Christ is referred to in scripture as a flock, a family and a body. As such, it can only have one head, and the head of the church is the Lord Jesus. Jesus rules His church through His Word and through His Spirit. And in the church, there is to be order. And part of that order requires there be a leader in the local church. That leader is the Pastor.

I must address one of the major problems in today's church. The problem is misplaced authority. Hear me, people of God. God knew what He was doing when He gave the church pastors after his own heart. He then placed in office the authority and responsibility to lead the church. This authority was not given to the board, the mission society, an auxiliary, ministry, member, association, or convention. He placed it in the office of the Pastor.

With that said, the office of Pastor deserves, demands and dictates that we, the members fall in line and follow him as he follows the Lord. One writer said, "It is the Pastors' commission to lead and it is the pews' commandment to follow." My interpretation of this statement is that I must be respectful of my pastor's rank. He deserves respectful obedience, cooperation and honor as he teaches, preaches, leads and loves God's Church.

I must be respectful of my pastor's relationship.

As I write this, I am celebrating my 34th preaching anniversary (the evening I preached my first sermon as a young man at the Fairview Missionary Baptist Church under the leadership of Dr. J. A. Reed, Jr.). As a son of the Fairview Baptist Church I am often called on by my Pastor to return home for a preaching or teaching assignment. Upon my return, I love talking to those who poured into my life as a boy growing up in the church. Some of those individuals include my Sunday school teachers, choir sponsors, children and youth workers, deacons and Baptist Training Union (B.T.U.) workers. The funny thing is every time I return and talk to them they only see that snotty nose boy. Over the years, Pastor Reed has begun to help the church to understand the relationship has changed not just for me, but for all his sons in the ministry that the church has been blessed to birth, mature, train and send out.

Pastor Reed understands that, while I am grateful and thankful for all the members of my home church sacrificed and poured into me to help me to become the person, teacher, preacher, and pastor that I am, once I accepted God's assignment to the office of Pastor our relationship was forever altered. God has laid upon me the responsibility and placed me in a position of authority over them. The assignment placed me in an office that should be honored and respected by others in the church. **1 Thessalonians 5:12-13 says, [12]"We ask you, brothers, to respect those who labor among you and are over you in the Lord and admonish you, [13]and to esteem them very highly in love because of their work. Be at peace among yourselves."** The phrase, *"to esteem them very highly,"* means they are *"to be held in the highest regard."*

Respect is something that should not be demanded. It is something earned over time. However, there is a certain amount of respect attached to the office of Pastor immediately. Over time, the pastor will earn more of your respect through sermons, teaching, preaching, ministering, comforting, supporting, and loving you.

Therefore…

✟ Teach your children to address him properly.

✟ Discipline yourself to treat him as the Pastor.

✟ Never be guilty of acting like "he's a man just like me, putting his pants on one leg at a time," because he isn't! Let me be clear, scripture isn't asking us to worship the man. However, God is calling us to be mindful and respectful of God by treating and responding to God's Pastor correctly because of his office.

✟ Remember pastors are not just "one of the guys".

✝ Your relationship to your pastor should be one of respect.

Let's review. We must "Be respectful of your Pastor's rank, be respectful of your Pastor's relationship, and finally, be respectful of your Pastor's responsibility.

I must be respectful of my pastor's responsibility.

Since God has placed and positioned Pastors as gifts in the lives of the people who sit in the pews of our churches, we must allow him to faithfully fulfill his God-given duty. The Apostle Paul writing to his young son in the ministry Timothy in **2 Timothy 4:1-5 said,** [1]**"I charge you in the presence of God and of Christ Jesus, who is to judge the living and the dead, and by his appearing and his kingdom:** [2]**preach the word; be ready in season and out of season; reprove, rebuke, and exhort, with complete patience and teaching.** [3]**For the time is coming when people will not endure sound teaching, but having itching ears they will accumulate for themselves teachers to suit their own passions,** [4]**and will turn away from listening to the truth and wander off into myths.** [5]**As for you, always be sober-minded, endure** *suffering, do the work of an evangelist, fulfill your ministry."* As Pastors, we are charged to tell the truth, the whole truth and nothing but the truth, so help us God!

The same preaching that will make one person shout will make another person pout. Now right here looks like a good place for me to sound a stern warning. When there is prayer in the pew, it will produce powerful proclamation from pastors, preachers and teachers that will wake up demons and devils that have laid dormant for years and even decades in the church. **Luke 4:31-37 says,** [31]*"And he went down to Capernaum, a city of Galilee. And he was teaching them on the Sabbath,* [32]*and they were astonished at his teaching, for his word possessed authority.* [33]*And in the synagogue there was a man who had the spirit of an unclean demon, and he cried out with a loud voice,* [34]*"Ha! What have you to do with us, Jesus of Nazareth? Have you come to destroy us? I know who you are—the Holy One of God."* [35]*But Jesus rebuked him, saying, "Be silent and come out of him!" And when the demon had thrown him down in their midst, he came out of him, having done him no harm.* [36]*And they were all amazed and said to one another, "What is this word? For with* *authority and power he commands the unclean spirits, and they come out!"* [37]*And reports about him went out into every place in the surrounding region.*"

As I travel across the country, I often share this passage with clergy and congregations and ask the question, "Have you ever wondered how long this man with this unclean spirit came to the temple and sat cute, calm and comfortable, while other came and preached without power?"

Be watchful and pray for your Pastor. Pray for his protection when the enemy attacks him through disgruntled, disagreeable, disrespectful and dishonoring people in the church. Your pastor shoulders a heavy responsibility in pastoring. His prayer is the people will follow him as He follows Christ. This is not always the case.

In 2008, my church had just begun a $2,000,000 campus project. The membership was growing exponentially. Our small groups were multiplying. Our mid-week worship experience was filled with not only members, but people from the community. It was then the enemy attacked with everything in his arsenal. It took years of fervent prayer for

God to reveal to me that, it wasn't anything I had done wrong, but instead what I had done right that provoked the attack. Whenever the Word of God is being preached, remember your Pastor loves you. Know that he has a burden for you and that his goal is to help you grow in the Lord. During times of blessing always be on guard, on the wall, watching and waiting on the attack of the enemy.

Your duty as a church is to gather around the preaching of the Word of God and to respond in humble obedience to the Word of God as it is delivered through the man of God from the house of God. Sometimes the word will be like Sunday dinner at grandma's house. Other times it will be like hospital food after a very long drawn out, life-threating and very difficult illness. However, it comes, remember that it comes from the mouth and heart of a man who loves you and has been sent by God to feed you and to lead you. Get behind the man of God; follow him and the Word he preaches. God will honor that kind of attitude!

Let's review again. We discussed the following things so far. 1. I must be mindful of my pastor. 2. I must be respectful of my pastor. And finally, 3. I must be faithful to my pastor.

3. I must be faithful to my pastor.

The author of the book of Hebrews is probably writing about leaders in the early church, such as the Apostles and others, who have already passed away or were martyred for their faith. The readers are challenged to consider the way they lived, the convictions they held and the example they left behind. They are also called to get in line behind them and live like they lived, do what they did and go after them faithfully to death.

I'm so very thankful that my childhood pastor is still with me. I can call him in good and bad times. He's my example, my friend, my mentor, and my pastor. In addition to Pastor Reed, there are several other pastors, men and women, along the way, who have made great contributions into my life, like the late Pastor C. C. Cooper, the late Pastor A. Glenn Woodberry, Pastor H.B. Charles Sr., Pastor E.K. Bailey, Pastor M. J. Williams, and not to mention my parents and grandparents. If you are blessed to still have your Pastor on this side of heaven be very thankful and if not, you are still able to honor their investment into your life by being faithful to their teaching even in their absence. The writer of the book of Hebrews teaches us to honor, love and respect the office of Pastor no matter what.

The writer of Hebrews reminds us to consider their way of life and imitate their faith. Before you can follow a man, you must look at his walk. This is not a call to criticism or to a judgmental attitude regarding your Pastor. If you look too closely at any man's life you will find many areas of fault and failure.

✦ This is a call for the church to take a close look at their Pastor.

✦ The church should watch him and imitate him as he walks with God by faith.

✦ The church needs to observe the convictions that grip his heart.

✦ The church needs to understand the fact that he carries you in his heart.

✦ The church needs to see the depth of his convictions.

✝ The church needs to realize the reality of his walk with God.

✝ The church needs to care about the commitment he demonstrates.

✝ The church needs to focus on the faithfulness that characterizes his life.

✝ The church needs to be bothered by the burden he carries for the church and for the Lord.

See these things and know he is God's man; he is worthy to be followed; and he worthy of respect because he is the spiritual leader of the church. Let his life serve as an example for your own walk with the Lord.

Hebrews 13:17 says, [13]"Obey your leaders and submit to them, for they are keeping watch over your souls, as those who will have to give an account. Let them do this with joy and not with groaning, for that would be of no advantage to you."

Have you ever worked on a job, a project or an assignment with a manager, co-worker or even a team member that just would not cooperate and complete the task? This person is always complaining, criticizing and causing confusing and chaos? If so, then you understand how working alongside someone would make an assignment, commission, and task, that could otherwise be pleasant, problematic. Likewise, those that sit comfortably in the pews of the church can easily make the pastor's assignment full of joy or full of sorrow; a great experience or a gloomy experience; a time of celebration of success or a time of chaos. I want to challenge you as we approach the end of this chapter, as a church and/or church member to get behind the man of God and follow him for the glory of God.

We talked about the benefits to the pastor when the people pray. So, what are the benefits of praying for your pastor for you?

Prayer in the Pews + Power in the Pulpit = Dedicated Lives

Prayer in the Pews + Power in the Pulpit = Transformed Lives

Prayer in the Pews + Power in the Pulpit = Prosperous Lives

Prayer in the Pews + Power in the Pulpit
= Equipped Lives

Always remember the success of Joshua and the army in the valley was determined by Moses' hands being held up on the hilltop. Moses needed an Aaron and a Hur. Will you commit to being Aaron or Hur today?

What Is Your Part?

If you have purchased this book, it is because you realize the importance of praying for your pastor. You understand his success is directly related to your survival. God has instituted a process that includes the proclamation of the gospel to the people. Your spiritual growth is directly related to being a part of a Bible-believing church where the Word of God is rightly divided.

The average expectation of the pastor is very high. Church members expect the pastor to bless their babies, marry their children, and bury their parents. However, they have been misguided in their expectation. While none of these things are wrong, they just are not the preacher's primary responsibility. The biblical mandate given to pastors is found in **II Timothy 4:2. "preach the word; be ready in season and out of season; reprove, rebuke, and exhort, with complete patience and teaching."** And as children of God we should want nothing to stand in the way of the Word going forth.

Over the next fifty-two weeks, we are asking you to make a commitment to join others across this city and this great state in praying the Word of God over our pastors. There are, included in this book, several different scripture-based ways to pray for the pastor. We encourage you to use them, as well as, write out your prayers for your pastor.

Romans 15:30-32 says, [30]"I appeal to you, brothers, by our Lord Jesus Christ and by the love of the Spirit, to strive together with me in your prayers to God on my behalf, [31]that I may be delivered from the unbelievers in Judea, and that my service for Jerusalem may be acceptable to the saints, [32]so that by God's will I may come to you with joy and be refreshed in your company."

Pray:
✞ Your pastor will be continuously covered in deep prayer support.

✞ Your pastor be delivered *(rescued)* from those that do not believe and those that try to stop the advancement of the gospel both from within and without.

✞ Your pastors' ministry will be pleasing in the eyes of the Lord and edifying to the saints.

✟ Your pastor is able to preach with joy in the midst of facing hardships.

✟ Your pastor is refreshed, renewed, and revived throughout his ministry as he seeks to do God's will.

✟ Your pastor is strengthened and sustained throughout his ministry as he seeks to do God's will.

COVERING THE ONE WHO COVERS YOU

Praying God's Word over your pastor is essential. If you have always wanted to pray for your pastor but you just weren't quite sure what to pray. Simply pray the Word of God. When you pray the Word of God you never must wonder if it is God's will. When you pray the Word of God you never must wonder if it is God's way. When you pray the Word of God you never must wonder what the result will be. The result will be God's man walking in His will and His way while doing His work.

So, let's try something. In this chapter, we want to show you how to pray for your pastor from the crown of his head to the soles of his feet.

Pray for your pastor's:

Head
Pray your pastor's head is filled with Godly thoughts that reveal the hidden treasures of His wisdom and knowledge that finds its foundation firmly fixed on his faith in Jesus Christ.

Colossians 2:3 [3]"in whom are hidden all the *treasures of wisdom and knowledge.*"

Colossians 2:5 [5]"For though I am absent in body, yet I am with you in spirit, rejoicing to see your good order and the firmness of your faith in Christ."

Colossians 3:2 [2] *"Set your minds* on things that are above, not on things that are on earth."

Eyes

Pray your pastor's eyes are focused upon Christ. That he looks to Jesus, the author and finisher of his faith, and never takes his eyes off Him.

Colossians 4:2-3 [2] "Continue steadfastly in prayer, *being watchful* in it with thanksgiving. [3] At the same time, pray also for us, that God may open to us a door for the word, to declare the mystery of Christ, on account of which I am in prison— "

Ears

Pray your pastor's ears are in tune to the Holy Spirit that produces a life that battles temptation, communes with Christ, examines himself, and continue to repent and believe day by day.

Colossians 3:10-14 [10] *"and have put on the new self, which is being renewed in knowledge* after the image of its creator. [11] Here there is not Greek and Jew, circumcised and uncircumcised, barbarian, Scythian, slave, free; but Christ is all, and in all. [12] Put on then, as God's chosen ones, holy and beloved, compassionate hearts, kindness, humility, meekness, and patience, [13] bearing with one another and, if one has a complaint against another, forgiving each other; as the Lord has forgiven you, so you also must forgive. [14] And above all these put on love, which binds everything together in perfect harmony."

Nose
Pray your pastor's nose is sensitive to heresy and sniffs it out quickly when it threatens the sheep.

Colossians 3:5-9 [5] *"Put to death therefore what is earthly in you*: sexual immorality, impurity, passion, evil desire, and covetousness, which is idolatry. [6] On account of these the wrath of God is coming. [7] In these you too once walked, when you were living in them. [8] But now you must put them all away: anger, wrath, malice, slander, and obscene talk from your mouth. [9] Do not lie to one another, seeing that you have put off the old self with its practices."

Mouth

Pray your pastor's mouth speaks the truth in love, in public and in private. He speaks clearly, consistently, and as simply as he possibly can even when talking, teaching or preaching about the most profound truths.

Colossians 1:28 [28] "Him we *proclaim*, warning everyone and teaching everyone with all wisdom, that we may present everyone mature in Christ."

Colossians 4:4 [4]" that I may make it clear, which is how I ought to *speak*."

Colossians 4:6 [6] "Let your *speech* always be gracious, seasoned with salt, so that you may know how you ought to *answer* each person."

Colossians 3:16 [16] "Let the *word* of Christ dwell in you richly, *teaching* and *admonishing* one another in all wisdom, *singing* psalms and hymns and spiritual songs…"

Heart

Pray your pastor's heart is wide open and he loves God and sinners, preaching passionately and visiting compassionately.

Colossians 2:2 (ESV) [2] that their *hearts* may be encouraged, being knit together in love, to reach all the riches of full assurance of understanding and the knowledge of God's mystery, which is Christ,

Colossians 3:12-16 [12] "Put on then, as God's chosen ones, holy and beloved, *compassionate hearts*, kindness, humility, meekness, and patience, [13] bearing with one another and, if one has a complaint against another, forgiving each other; as the Lord has forgiven you, so you also must forgive. [14] And above all these put on love, which binds everything together in perfect harmony. [15] *And let the peace of Christ rule in your hearts*, to which indeed you were called in one body. And be thankful. [16] ...with thankfulness in your *hearts* to God."

Hands

Pray your pastor's hands are determined, persevering, and resolute, even in times of fierce opposition, tremendous temptation, discouraging day and long days of labor.

Colossians 3:17 ¹⁷ "And whatever you *do, in word or deed, do* everything in the name of the Lord Jesus, giving thanks to God the Father through him."

Colossians 1:29 ²⁹ "*For this I toil*, struggling with all his energy that he powerfully works within me.

Feet
Pray your pastor's feet walk the narrow way, turning not to the right or left.

Colossians 1:10 ¹⁰ "so as to *walk in a manner worthy of the Lord*, fully pleasing to him, bearing fruit in every good work and increasing in the knowledge of God."

Colossians 2:6-7 ⁶ "Therefore, as you received Christ Jesus the Lord, *so walk in him*, ⁷ rooted and built up in him and established in the faith, just as you were taught, abounding in thanksgiving."

Colossians 4:5 ⁵ "*Walk in wisdom* toward outsiders, making the best use of the time."

Pastor G's Five Fav Finger Prayer for Pastors

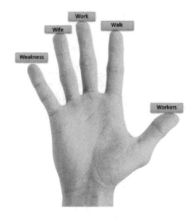

Thumb – Pray that the God of the harvest, convict, change and charge willing workers who are equipped with the Word to be become willing workers in ministry. (Luke 10:2)

Pointer – Pray that God will allow your Pastor to walk in kindness, forgiveness and the likeness of Christ Jesus. (Ephesians 4:32-51)

Middle – Pray that God will prepare your Pastor to preach in season and out of season. (2Timothy 4:1-5)

Ring – Pray that God will protect your Pastor's marriage from the enemy causing their marriage to be long, loving and full of laughter. (Ephesians 5:25)

Pinky – Pray that God will build a wall of protection from the world, the flesh and the devil and that he will be able to recognize every plot and plan. (Ephesians 6:10-13)

Pray that/for your pastor's

- Relationship with God will be marked by a sense of awe, reverence and respect.

- Love for God will grow deeper each day.

- Character and integrity as a man of God.

- Passion and pursuit for Jesus.

- Obedience to the Holy Spirit and that he will be continually be filled and refreshed.

- Marriage would be exemplary.

- Fatherhood, that he honors and loves his children.

- Hurt, headaches, and heartbreak will heal.

- Ministry will be full of joy.

- Protection from the evil one, evil doers and evil.

- Put on the whole armor of God.

- Relationships, friendships and partnerships

.
- Life would be balanced spiritually, physically, emotionally, relationally, and occupationally
- Call to as a pastor-teacher.

- Commitment to the great commission and great commandment.

- Prayer life will be regular.

- Worship will be done in spirit and truth.

- Will write the vision and make it plain.

- Mind will be transformed.

- Ministry friends will understand the privilege to walk alongside of him.

- Ministry enemies, that God will expose them and cut them down like the grass.

- Trust in God would be in all his ways.

PRAYING GOD'S WORD
BIBLICAL EXAMPLES

Scripture Reference No.1:

2 Timothy 2:23-26 says, [23] "Have nothing to do with foolish, ignorant controversies; you know that they breed quarrels. [24] And the Lord's servant must not be quarrelsome but kind to everyone, able to teach, patiently enduring evil, [25] correcting his opponents with gentleness. God may perhaps grant them repentance leading to a knowledge of the truth, [26] and they may come to their senses and escape from the snare of the devil, after being captured by him to do his will."

Day 1: Pray for your pastor that he has nothing to do with foolish people, plots, and polemics knowing these things produce quarrels and the Lord's servant-leader must never be petulant, petty, or prideful. Pray your Pastor will not allow the evil one, evil people or evil things to cause him to stoop to their level, being a living testimony, rising above them that want you to hang out below.

Day 2: Pray for your pastor because we have learned through, "Praying for our Pastors," that anointed teaching and preaching comes at a great cost to the Pastor, the Pastor's wife, children, grandchildren, friendships and other very important relationships that are vital for a healthy, whole and holy person. Pray God will protect your Pastor's most vital relationships in the fight over the souls, spirits and salvation of His people.

Day 3: Pray for your pastor because as God's herald, the enemy wants to ambush the messenger of God, so the people of God will not receive the Word of God. Each time your Pastor stands to preach or teach the Word of God, it does not come without fierce obstruction, objection and opposition from Satan. Pray your Pastor will overcome the enemy by being kind to everyone, continuing to teach and patiently enduring evil and correcting with gentleness.

Day 4: Pray for your pastor because to truly be a "pastor after God's own heart..." the Pastor must be God's "servant" Servant in the Greek means "slave." A slave has no will of his own. He is totally under the command of his master. Look at it this way, as unbelievers we were slaves to sin but now as believers we are slaves to God. Pray your Pastor accepts the role of a "bond-servant," who has been set free to serve God the way He desires, deserves, and demands.

Day 5: Pray for your pastor because commitment to preaching and teaching God's Word, doesn't exclude your pastor from spiritual warfare but includes him. Pray that your Pastor will not be blindsided by the temptation of being more concerned with winning an argument rather than winning willing souls, defending himself rather than allowing God to be their defender, and being preoccupied with Facebook rather than God's Book

Praying Gods Word:
Father God, help my Pastor be strong in Your mighty power, staying vigilant, being watchful and being prayerful as teacher

and preacher of Your Word. Father, keep my Pastor from the engagement or involvement of, in or with foolish, undisciplined, ignorant and stupid debates, arguments, quarrels or fights which are all thing a servant of the Lord must not engage in, strive in, or debate. Allow my Pastor through Your Power to be kind to everyone, be able to teach, and be patient with difficult people, gently instructing and correcting those who oppose the truth in hope that God will change those people's hearts and they will learn the truth. 2 Timothy 2: 23-25

Scripture Reference No.2
Hebrews 12:1-3 says, [1] "Therefore, since we are surrounded by so great a cloud of witnesses, let us also lay aside every weight, and sin which clings so closely, and let us run with endurance the race that is set before us, [2] looking to Jesus, the founder and perfecter of our faith, who for the joy that was set before him endured the cross, despising the shame, and is seated at the right hand of the throne of God. [3]Consider him who endured from sinners

such hostility against himself, so that you may not grow weary or fainthearted.

Day 1: Pray for your pastor because perfection isn't a prerequisite for preaching or pastoring. In fact, sin is found in the person in the pulpit, just as it is found in the people in the pews. In other words, where you sit in church doesn't exclude you from the struggle and weight of sin. Sin is described as ANYTHING that has more of you or a stronger hold on you than God does. Hebrews 12:1b tells us to, "let us also lay aside every weight and sin which clings so closely..." We all have a problem with sin, but God through Jesus Christ has already ensured us victory over all encumbrances of life and entanglements of sin that cause the courageous to become discouraged.

Day 2: Pray for your pastor because they are people too. Like us, they struggle with endurance as they run their race, struggling and contending for the cause of Christ in a critical and callus world. The ministry of the Pastor includes seasons of smooth sailing and moments of mounting misery, massive mistakes and missteps in ministry. These are the times the Hebrew writer encourages us to pray for that our Pastors "… run with endurance the race that is set before us…" Hebrews 12:1c Pray your Pastor runs long, hard, and steady, with patience, enduring the race for the glory of God!

Day 3: Pray for your pastor because one momentary distraction, disappointment or discouragement during the race could result in devastating detours and disastrous danger for both the Pastor and the people. The Hebrew writer once again cautions us to, "to run the race looking to Jesus…" Hebrews 12:2a Pray that your Pastor keeps dedicated, determined and diligent watch on Jesus.

Day 4: Pray for your pastor because undisciplined eyes lead to defeats, unfocused eyes lead to failure and unsteady eyes lead to stumbling. The writer reminds us to keep looking, longing and running for Jesus "run the race looking to…the founder (author) of our faith …" Hebrews 12:2b Pray that your Pastor's eyes will get off and stay off other racers, keep from judging his race against someone else's race, and faithfully focus on Jesus who calls the race, watches over the race, judges the race and will ultimately reward the racers.

Day 5: Pray for your pastor because Jesus has finished and fixed the race He has given him to run eagerly, enthusiastically, fervently and faithfully. Hebrews 12: 2b "run the race looking to...the perfecter (finisher) of our faith..." Jesus Christ has already finished the race and if we faithfully focus and follow Him, He knows the pitfalls, pressures, and the path that we will encounter and He has already fixed the race for us. Pray that your Pastor realizes that if he fixes his focus on the Finisher of the race, the Finisher will also become the Fixer of the race and the victory is already won.

Praying God's Word:

Father help our Pastor keep his eyes focused on Jesus! Life is full of things that would cause distraction, discouragement and disappointments and many times we lose heart and focus. When those times come in the life of our Pastor, please remind him of the huge crowd of witnesses in his life to this faith walk. Encourage him to strip off and lay aside every weight that slows and weighs him down, especially the sin that so easily trips him up. And let him run with endurance and perseverance the race that You have set before him as Your mouthpiece, Your preacher and Your teacher. We pray that You, Father, will give him spiritual blinders that will allow him to only look unto Jesus, the author and perfector and the champion of our faith. I pray he will look to The One who endured the cross, its scorn, its shame and is now seated in the place of honor beside Your throne. We pray our Pastor will never become weary, worn or worried, but through Your Word will be reminded there is a great reward for those who will stay in the fight, stay faithful, and stay focused until the end. Scripture: Hebrews 12:1-3

Additional Daily Prayer:

Father, we lift our pastors in prayer and ask You to help them to know Him (Jesus) and the power of His resurrection, that they may share in His sufferings, and become like Him in His death. For this reason, we pray since we know of their faith in the Lord Jesus and their love toward all the saints, remembering them in our prayers. We join an army of others, asking that You, God of our Lord Jesus Christ, the Father of glory, may give them the Spirit of wisdom and of revelation so that they may know You better. Philippians 3:10 & Ephesians 1:15-17

Saturday Evening Prayer:

Father, this has been an incredible week, with all of life's demands, distractions, disappointments and unexpected disturbances that seek to steal the most valuable entrustment which is TIME. We lift our Pastor and other Pastors to You, who have faithfully fought against the enemy just to pray, prepare, prep, practice, preach and to proclaim a life-changing Word. We pray that our Pastor's message is plain, portable and profitable and not filled with enticing, persuasive, and clever words. And let what is done in our pulpits be a demonstration of the Spirit and of power, so our faith might not rest in human wisdom but in Your Power. We pray You, God, the source of hope, will fill our Pastor with joy and peace as he trusts in You, so that he will overflow with confident hope through the power of the Holy Spirit. I Corinthians 2:4-5 & Romans 15:13 (ESV & NLT)

This ends the biblical instructions why we should pray for our pastors. Now is the time to put action to what we have learned. My prayer is you will pray the Word of God over your pastor using the Scriptures provided weekly. My desire is that you will even write down your prayers in the space provided as a reference tool you can refer to for years to come.

My prayer is that, not only will you pray, but you will also encourage others to pray with you. Make praying for your pastor a part of your intercessory prayer group. Make praying for your pastor a part of your small group Bible study. Make praying for your pastor a part of your weekly deacon meeting. Make praying for your pastor a part of your morning coffee break with your co-workers. Make praying for your pastor a part of your family devotion.

52 WEEK PRAYER GUIDE

Week One

Luke 18:1 And he told them a parable to the effect that they ought always to pray and not lose heart.

Week Two

Romans 15:30-32 [30] I appeal to you, brothers, by our Lord Jesus Christ and by the love of the Spirit, to strive together with me in your prayers to God on my behalf, [31] that I may be delivered from the unbelievers in Judea, and that my service for Jerusalem may be acceptable to the saints, [32] so that by God's will I may come to you with joy and be refreshed in your company.

Week Three

Hebrews 12:1 Therefore, since we are surrounded by so great a cloud of witnesses, let us also lay aside every weight, and sin which clings so closely, and let us run with endurance the race that is set before us,

Week Four

2 Timothy 2:24-25a And the Lord's servant must not be quarrelsome but kind to everyone, able to teach, patiently enduring evil, correcting his opponents with gentleness.

Week Five

Titus 1:9 He must hold firm to the trustworthy word as taught, so that he may be able to give instruction in sound doctrine and also to rebuke those who contradict it.

Week Six

James 3:13 Who is wise and understanding among you? By his good conduct let him show his works in the meekness of wisdom.

Week Seven

Romans 12:9 Let love be genuine. Abhor what is evil; hold fast to what is good.

Week Eight

I Timothy 5:21 In the presence of God and of Christ Jesus and of the elect angels I charge you to keep these rules without prejudging, doing nothing from partiality.

Week Nine

2 Corinthians 2:17 For we are not, like so many, peddlers of God's word, but as men of sincerity, as commissioned by God, in the sight of God we speak in Christ.

Week Ten

II Timothy 2:1-2 You then, my child, be strengthened by the grace that is in Christ Jesus, 2 and what you have heard from me in the presence of many witnesses entrust to faithful men, who will be able to teach others also.

Week Eleven

I Corinthians 15:58 Therefore, my beloved brothers, be steadfast, immovable, always abounding in the work of the Lord, knowing that in the Lord your labor is not in vain.

Week Twelve

Galatians 6:9 And let us not grow weary of doing good, for in due season we will reap, if we do not give up.

Week Thirteen

Philippian 4:19 And my God will supply every need of yours according to his riches in glory in Christ Jesus.

Week Fourteen

Numbers 6:24-26 The Lord bless you and keep you; the Lord make his face to shine upon you and be gracious to you; the Lord lift up his countenance upon you and give you peace.

Week Fifteen

I Timothy 2:1-3 First of all, then, I urge that supplications, prayers, intercessions, and thanksgivings be made for all people, for kings and all who are in high positions, that we may lead a peaceful and quiet life, godly and dignified in every way. This is good, and it is pleasing in the sight of God our Savior.

Week Sixteen

I Peter 3:12 For the eyes of the Lord are on the righteous, and his ears are open to their prayer. But the face of the Lord is against those who do evil."

Week Seventeen

Proverbs 4:6-7 Do not forsake her, and she will keep you; love her, and she will guard you. The beginning of wisdom is this: Get wisdom, and whatever you get, get insight.

Week Eighteen

Romans 15:13 May the God of hope fill you with all joy and peace in believing, so that by the power of the Holy Spirit you may abound in hope.

Week Nineteen

2 Timothy 2:15 Do your best to present yourself to God as one approved, a worker who has no need to be ashamed, rightly handling the word of truth.

Week Twenty

Isaiah 40:31 but they who wait for the LORD shall renew their strength; they shall mount up with wings like eagles; they shall run and not be weary; they shall walk and not faint.

Week Twenty-One

Jeremiah 29:12-14 Then you will call upon me and come and pray to me, and I will hear you. You will seek me and find me, when you seek me with all your heart. I will be found by you, declares the Lord, and I will restore your fortunes and gather you from all the nations and all the places where I have driven you, declares the Lord, and I will bring you back to the place from which I sent you into exile.

Week Twenty-Two

Jeremiah 9:23-24 Thus says the Lord: "Let not the wise man boast in his wisdom, let not the mighty man boast in his might, let not the rich man boast in his riches, but let him who boasts boast in this, that he understands and knows me, that I am the LORD who practices steadfast love, justice, and righteousness in the earth. For in these things I delight, declares the Lord."

Week Twenty-Three

I Peter 3:15 but in your hearts honor Christ the Lord as holy, always being prepared to make a defense to anyone who asks you for a reason for the hope that is in you; yet do it with gentleness and respect,

Week Twenty-Four

2 Peter 3:17 You therefore, beloved, knowing this beforehand, take care that you are not carried away with the error of lawless people and lose your own stability.

Week Twenty-Five

Romans 10:12 For there is no distinction between Jew and Greek; for the same Lord is Lord of all, bestowing his riches on all who call on him.

Week Twenty-Six

Ephesians 6:18 Praying at all times in the Spirit, with all prayer and supplication. To that end keep alert with all perseverance, making supplication for all the saints,

Week Twenty-Seven

Isaiah 43:2 When you pass through the waters, I will be with you; and through the rivers, they shall not overwhelm you; when you walk through fire you shall not be burned, and the flame shall not consume you.

Week Twenty-Eight

I Corinthians 9:14 In the same way, the Lord commanded that those who proclaim the gospel should get their living by the gospel.

Week Twenty-Nine

Colossians 4:3 At the same time, pray also for us, that God may open to us a door for the word, to declare the mystery of Christ, on account of which I am in prison—

Week Thirty

Ephesians 6:19 and also for me, that words may be given to me in opening my mouth boldly to proclaim the mystery of the gospel,

Week Thirty-One

Isaiah 11:2 And the Spirit of the LORD shall rest upon him, the Spirit of wisdom and understanding, the Spirit of counsel and might, the Spirit of knowledge and the fear of the LORD.

Week Thirty-Two

Deuteronomy 6:5 You shall love the LORD your God with all your heart and with all your soul and with all your might.

Week Thirty-Three

Ephesians 1:15-17 For this reason, because I have heard of your faith in the Lord Jesus and your love toward all the saints, I do not cease to give thanks for you, remembering you in my prayers, that the God of our Lord Jesus Christ, the Father of glory, may give you the Spirit of wisdom and of revelation in the knowledge of him.

Week Thirty-Four

Ephesians 6:10 Finally, be strong in the Lord and in the strength of his might.

Week Thirty-Five

Ephesians 6:11 Put on the whole armor of God, that you may be able to stand against the schemes of the devil.

Week Thirty-Six

Philippians 4:6 do not be anxious about anything, but in everything by prayer and supplication with thanksgiving let your requests be made known to God.

Week Thirty-Seven

I Peter 5:5 Likewise, you who are younger, be subject to the elders. Clothe yourselves, all of you, with humility toward one another, for "God opposes the proud but gives grace to the humble."

Week Thirty-Eight

Galatians 5:16 But I say, walk by the Spirit, and you will not gratify the desires of the flesh.

Week Thirty-Nine

Psalms 91:9-10 Because you have made the Lord your dwelling place—the Most High, who is my refuge no evil shall be allowed to befall you, no plague come near your tent.

Week Forty

Galatians 6:14 But far be it from me to boast except in the cross of our Lord Jesus Christ, by which the world has been crucified to me, and I to the world.

Week Forty-One

Psalms 69:32 When the humble see it they will be glad; you who seek God, let your hearts revive.

Week Forty-Two

Galatians 5:22-23 But the fruit of the Spirit is love, joy, peace, patience, kindness, goodness, faithfulness, gentleness, self-control; against such things there is no law.

Week Forty-Three

Colossians 4:5 Walk in wisdom toward outsiders, making the best use of the time.

Week Forty-Four

Colossians 2:2-3 that their hearts may be encouraged, being knit together in love, to reach all the riches of full assurance of understanding and the knowledge of God's mystery, which is Christ, in whom are hidden all the treasures of wisdom and knowledge.

Week Forty-Five

Psalms 145:14-15 The Lord upholds all who are falling and raises up all who are bowed down. The eyes of all look to you, and you give them their food in due season.

Week Forty-Six

Romans 14:19 So then let us pursue what makes for peace and for mutual upbuilding.

Week Forty-Seven

Proverbs 3:5-7 Trust in the Lord with all your heart, and do not lean on your own understanding. In all your ways acknowledge him, and he will make straight your paths. Be not wise in your own eyes; fear the Lord, and turn away from evil.

Week Forty-Eight

John 15:4-5 Abide in me, and I in you. As the branch cannot bear fruit by itself, unless it abides in the vine, neither can you, unless you abide in me. I am the vine; you are the branches. Whoever abides in me and I in him, he it is that bears much fruit, for apart from me you can do nothing.

Week Forty-Nine

Colossians 3:12 Put on then, as God's chosen ones, holy and beloved, compassionate hearts, kindness, humility, meekness, and patience.

Week Fifty

Romans 12:1 I appeal to you therefore, brothers, by the mercies of God, to present your bodies as a living sacrifice, holy and acceptable to God, which is your spiritual worship.

Week Fifty-One

Philippians 2:1-3 So if there is any encouragement in Christ, any comfort from love, any participation in the Spirit, any affection and sympathy, complete my joy by being of the same mind, having the same love, being in full accord and of one mind. Do nothing from selfish ambition or conceit, but in humility count others more significant than yourselves.

Week Fifty-Two

Luke 9:23-24 And he said to all, "If anyone would come after me, let him deny himself and take up his cross daily and follow me. For whoever would save his life will lose it, but whoever loses his life for my sake will save it.

WHAT CAN YOU DO?

Does your church currently have an Intercessory Prayer Ministry? Have you considered adding a component to your men's group or women's group that includes holding up the hands of the pastor? **Exodus 17:11-12 says,** *"Whenever Moses held up his hand, Israel prevailed, and whenever he lowered his hand, Amalek prevailed. But Moses' hands grew weary, so they took a stone and put it under him, and he sat on it, while Aaron and Hur held up his hands, one on one side, and the other on the other side. So, his hands were steady until the going down of the sun."* As stated previously, your pastor needs you. He needs you to hold up his arms. He needs you to make a concerted, concentrated and committed effort to pray for him.

So, I'll ask you again does your church or Bible Study group include a component that prays for your pastor. If not, consider adding a ministry that prays specifically for the pastor. This would be a perfect addition to your current prayer strategy. Daily there are many things that come up against the man of God to distract him from hearing the voice of the Lord. Each and every time he prepares to stand there are missiles launched that has a specific mission to take out the man of God. He is the target. The enemy does not want him to complete his assignment. The enemy does not want him to help make disciples. The enemy does not want him to stand and proclaim the good news of Jesus Christ.

One of the ways he can counter these attacks is through the prayers that are being lifted to God by the people he has been assigned to cover. Do you have any idea how much better a shepherd your pastor would be if he was being constantly covered in prayer?

Pastor G Ministries is available to come to your church and meet with your prayer team and help them to understand not only the way the pastor benefits from the prayers of the righteous; but also, how the member benefits from praying for the pastor. No army has ever been successful without a battle plan. God has given us the strategy for victory in His Word. All we have to do as children of God is follow through with the plan.

Tool for Starting a Pastors' Prayer Ministry in Your Church

Example taken from the:
Greater Bethel Baptist Church
Praying for our Pastors Ministry
Created: May 27, 2014

Our Ministry: Praying for our Pastors

Our Core Value(s): Belonging & Serving

Our Purpose: To produce and promote prayer in the pews that increases power in the pulpits that produces powerful people for the work in the kingdom.

Our Mission: The mission is to first, glorify God by praying for the office of the Pastor and the gift we receive from the Pastor. We also want to undergird the Pastor in the preaching and teaching ministry to ensure there is ample power in the pulpit in my church and in pulpits across this country.

Our Commitment: As an active member, I will commit to praying for my Pastor and other Pastor during my private devotion.

Our Schedule:
✞ Weekly intercessory prayer will be offered up for my pastor, as well as, other pastors around the country in the areas of personal, professional, relational, spiritual, financial, and congregational growth.

✞ Monthly intercessory prayer will be offered up for pastors on scheduled "Praying for our Pastors" gatherings with Pastor G Ministries.

✞ Twice a year pastors, marriages, families, ministries and churches will be lifted in intense prayer through our annual prayer and fasting days, prayer retreat, and prayer breakfast.

Here is an example of a form you can sit down with your pastor to find out his specific prayer needs.

When is your preaching anniversary date?
___ / ___ / _____
When is your ordination date? ___ / ___ / _____

What is your pastoral anniversary date?
___ / ___ / _____
How many years? _____
When is your wedding anniversary?
___ / ___ / _____
How many children do you have? _____.
What are their names and ages?

Name:	Age:	Name:	Age:

October is National Clergy Appreciation month. Would you be willing to give me a day where we could hold a prayer service to pray for you and your spouse specifically?
If so when? ___ / ___ / _____

Are there any particularly difficult days that you would like to share with me that we may pray for you?

_____

_____

Are there any initial prayer requests that you would like us to begin to pray for?

Intercessory Prayer Needs:

Personal needs:

Professional needs:

Relational needs:

Spiritual needs:

Financial needs:

Congregational needs:

 Reverend Teron V. Gaddis is the Senior Pastor-Teacher of the Greater Bethel Baptist Church in Oklahoma City, Oklahoma. Pastor Gaddis is one of today's most gifted communicators who offers a clear, contemporary and creative teaching style. He has a passion for making the complex simple as he speaks truth to people in ways they can understand and apply to their everyday lives.

Pastor G's preaching style includes careful exposition of Scripture, combined with his signature detailed stories from contemporary life that enrich the sermon and encourages the congregation.

Pastor G is passionate about changed lives, whether a person is coming to Christ for the very first time or rededicating their life for the 100th time, nothing excites him more than to see people began to live fully committed and capable followers of Jesus Christ. His goal in ministry is to please his heavenly Father and to be a faithful steward of the lives that have been entrusted into his hands.

Pastor G has been married to Janice for thirty years and the two of them have five children and ten grandchildren.

After 34 years in ministry and 25 years of pastoring, Pastor G continues to be a leading voice in innovation, inspiration and influence

Small Group Bible Studies
Written by Pastor Teron V. Gaddis
(All studies available for reproduction.
Send request to chiefofstaff@pastorgministries.com)

My Belief Matters

An eight-week study on basic Baptist doctrine with sermon outlines and weekly Bible Study lessons.

My Belief Will Dictate My Behavior

A ten-week study on the life-changing power of the Word of God and how your belief will change your behavior. Includes Sunday sermon outlines, Wednesday Bible study outlines and small group lessons

From Possession to Possession
21 Day Fast
A daily study of the book of Joshua designed to be incorporated with a time of prayer and fasting.